Archives of the Air

JOHN MORGAN

John Morgan [signature]

salmonpoetry

Published in 2015 by
Salmon Poetry
Cliffs of Moher, County Clare, Ireland
Website: www.salmonpoetry.com
Email: info@salmonpoetry.com

Copyright © John Morgan, 2015

ISBN 978-1-910669-11-2

All rights reserved. No part of this publication may be reproduced or transmitted in any form or by any means, electronic or mechanical, including photography, recording, or any information storage or retrieval system, without permission in writing from the publisher. The book is sold subject to the condition that it shall not, by way of trade or otherwise, be lent, resold or otherwise circulated without the publisher's prior consent in any form of binding or cover other than that in which it is published and without a similar condition, including this condition, being imposed on the subsequent purchaser.

COVER ARTWORK: "An Intimate Gathering," fiber art by *Karin Franzen*.
Commissioned by Bill Stringer in memory of his wife, Sandra.
Photograph by Eric Nancarrow.
COVER DESIGN & TYPESETTING: *Siobhán Hutson*
Printed in Ireland by Sprint Print

for Nancy again, in our fiftieth year

Acknowledgments

Thanks to the following publications where some of these poems first appeared:

ASCENT: "November Surprise"
CIRQUE: "American Taliban," "Arrival," "Firestorm," and "Two Views of the Wreckage"
CLOVER: "From a Journal"
THE COLORADO REVIEW: "Analects of the Red Canoe"
GREAT RIVER REVIEW: "Archives of the Air"
IN LIKE COMPANY (anthology): "A Renaissance Altarpiece"
MĀNOA: "Above the Tanana: For Jerry Cable"
THE NORTH AMERICAN REVIEW: "Postcard from Nancy"
THE NORTHERN REVIEW: "The Unnamed Lake"
SALT RIVER REVIEW: "Psalm (After Nietzsche)" and "The Unsafe House"
SUBTROPICS: "Vision"
WORDS AND PICTURES: "Mt. Tamalpais"

I also wish to thank the Rasmuson Foundation for its generous support. And my special thanks to Jessie Lendennie for her valued friendship and to Siobhán Hutson for her great work.

Also my continuing gratitude to these friends for their help as the poems in this book came together: Jean Anderson, Derick Burleson, Peggy Shumaker, Marjorie Cole, Kimberly Cornwall, Burns Cooper, Cynthia Hardy, Susheila Khera, John Kooistra, John Reinhard, and Linda Schandelmeier.

Contents

I. ARCHIVES

ARCHIVES OF THE AIR	11
NOVEMBER SURPRISE	13
FROM A JOURNAL	14
VISION	16
A HEAD	17
ABOVE THE TANANA: FOR MALI GERGELY	18
ALIEN CORN	20
THE GOOD LIFE (A DREAM)	21
UNDER YUCATAN	22
MT. TAMALPAIS	24
THE ATTACK	26
THE UNSAFE HOUSE	27
HOMELESS IN SEATTLE	28
CELESTIAL FIRESTORM	29
POSTCARD FROM NANCY	30

II. ANALECTS (a gathering of literary fragments)

ANALECTS OF THE RED CANOE	35

III. HISTORIES

ELISABETH VIGÉE-LEBRUN: SELF PORTRAIT	45
"A-CRANBERRYING"	48
A RENAISSANCE ALTARPIECE	49
COUNTING CARIBOU—PRUDHOE BAY, ALASKA	50
ABOVE THE TANANA: FOR JERRY CABLE	51
ASK LOUISE	56
INTO MY HEAD	58
TWO VIEWS OF THE WRECKAGE	59
SOUNDS IN A FOREST	60
AMERICAN TALABAN	61
THE ASSIGNMENT	63
THE UNNAMED LAKE	65
DENALI PARK FALL DRIVE-THROUGH	66
PSALM: AFTER NIETZSCHE	67

I.
ARCHIVES

ARCHIVES OF THE AIR

This guy who knows more about cranes
than they know about themselves
    (because their brains
are thumbnail small) explains that the sandhill's

call—a loud rattle and a squeak—comes not from
one crane's beak but two, the male's note answered
    by his mate's.
Also, he states, when one of them croaks,

the survivor often hangs around for months
and mopes, and here he relates the story of
    a grieving
female in the DMZ between the

two Koreas, rescued at great risk
by South Korean troops and shipped to him in
    Maryland, though
the law forbids it, yet she arrived

safely and briefly joined his local set.
He's the one who, using ultra-lightweight
    planes with crane
insignias, teaches home-bred whooping

cranes to migrate. Whoopers are less endangered
thanks to him. He raised one female from
    the egg and,
wearing a crane costume and pointing his beak

to the sky while flapping his fake crane wings
and jumping up and down, coached her in
    the mating dance,
but when someone jokes, "Sounds like a fine

romance," our self-styled *crane-iac* shakes his head.
"Totally boring," since he had to be
    outfitted and at
her beck and call whenever she wanted to ball.

Nestlings keep their distinctive peep for
a year, though fully grown by then,
    so the family unit
holds through one full cycle of migration.

They ride the mile-high winds with a sixth
magnetic sense that returns them to the acre
    where they began,
a skill that puzzles even our crane man.

As we circle the field, watching through our scopes
the long-legged, red-capped semi-prehistoric crew,
    scuffles and
skirmishes erupt and feathers ruffle,

some lower their shoulders and crane their necks
suggesting flight. Some glide in low and land
    while others take off.
"If the chill is strong," he says, "perhaps tonight."

NOVEMBER SURPRISE
Fairbanks, Alaska

Ten below and ice-mist on the river
when "Oh," she says, "a butterfly!" as it
comes wobbling from the sun-room, settles
on the floor. We offer sugar water
in a spoon and watch its sucking tube unroll.
It sips, then flutters to the windowsill
and folds its scalloped wings against the chill.

By noon, bright sun, and full of spunk it beats
against the glass, in love with light. The ground
outside, a spanking white, looks welcoming.
Its wings, like paisley, red and brown, quiver
as it paws the pane, embodiment of
summer in late fall, cold-blooded thing,
whose hopes will never be this young again.

FROM A JOURNAL

Note: this poem and the two that follow are based on the journal I kept while serving as writer-in-residence at Denali National Park

Woke to heavy rain, low clouds,
the wet-rag sky wrung out
with little hope for change. But hey—

it's the park. Let's go.
And driving toward Eielson, the rain
does change—to snow.

There on a hillside, a mother
grizzly playing with her cub—
delighted with each other

and by the frosty white,
they roll and wrestle in it.
At Eielson, a snowball fight

pits kids against the giddy bus
dispatcher. We take a hike.
And later hike again near

Stony Creek, noting a mound
of grizzly scat beside
a stretch of torn up ground

where the ravenous bear
rummaged turf for
ground squirrels—earth

gouged, mined, ripped, rocks
tossed aside like
ping-pong balls, a thorough

thrashing of the region.
Wild nature on a tear
alters our perspective (after

the playful grappling of
mother and cub) on the crushing
strength and menace of a bear.

VISION

Followed a fox toward Polychrome Pass.
Red smudged
with black along its lean rib-cage,

it rubs its muzzle on a former meal,
ignores the
impatient poet on its tail.

Then nearing the overlook, sun shearing
through low clouds
transmutes the view to glitter. Everything's

golden, scintillant. I feel like a seedpod wafted
into space and
check my shaky hands on the steering wheel.

As the road crests over its top, boundaries
dissolve. Beside that
sheer intractable edge, I greet my radiant center,

discharge all my terms. How easy it seems
to channel between
worlds, my old self dying into a new,

with nothing firm to hold me here
but love. And that's
what nature has it in its power to do.

THE HEAD

Nature, great creator, full
of invention, fabrication.

Day ten, went for a good-by look
to the bank of the East Fork, glacial

river, thick gray water. Suddenly
a head pokes up. A fish, an

otter? There's no telling—
barely seen, it vanishes.

Dream? Illusion? Was it
just a mental bubble?

But then that same queer
head pops up again, followed

by the long-necked mottled
body of a duck. Duck in a panic,

flapping, paddling, launches
a mad-dash for shore, and seems

about to make it when
the silted channel swallows it again.

ABOVE THE TANANA:
FOR MALI GERGELY (1885-1966)

Note: The Tanana River rises in western Canada and flows through central Alaska before joining the Yukon. Several poems in this collection are set on a ledge overlooking the river, with a long view south to the Alaska Range.

The fire that over-wintered under snow
spills smoke in front of the front range, stunts
the view, a ghostly scrim on which I picture you,

a rush of life drawn from your years of struggle
toward belief. A swallowtail flutters past,
and catkins float from cottonwoods like

wintry rabbit's feet. Searching the web the
other day I found your bio, mistranslated
by machine. It called you "he" and fumbled

every verb. Still, I learned you studied art
in Paris, probed the folk-ways of
your native Hungary and when the

democratic revolution crashed you wrote:
"Each soul must find its path alone, since
all collective deeds dead-end in flames."

Pasque flowers gone, no roses yet. The slough
has taken half of its guarding island out and
the restless flow's eroding south. Exiled to

Austria, you fled again from Hitler's gang
and wound up in New York beside the El.
Up two flights, a reek of turpentine and oils

(at nine, I shrink back, pinch my nose),
you perched among us in a flowered smock,
painting and smoking Camels without stop,

the ashes drooping, falling to your lap.
You lined the colors up and prepped
our canvases, then let us go our way,

but when I needed help—a mallard's wing,
the tint of blue for sky—you sensed my wish
to paint elation not just bird, and conjured up

a lilting pool of sky. Then after class,
unknown to us, you plumbed another art.
A raven's shadow drifting past, a kestrel's

sharp alarm. This braded glacial river's not
a place you'd ever want to take a dunking in.
I Googled up the grave in Budapest

that holds your ashes and pays tribute to
your works: the textiles, poems, paintings,
and the celebrated novel of your later years.

Ash—the smoking got you in the end. You said,
"I wouldn't want to be among the blessed
unless the animals can be there too."

ALIEN CORN

My Aunt Ruth's shucking corn with us. It's odd.
She takes a knife and shears the kernels off, to
fry them like her mother used to do,
but I say, "No. We're cooking on-the-cob,"

and wake up knowing that my aunt's long dead.
Then lines recur from Keats' great ode where corn
and Ruth are linked, when "sick for home she stood
in tears…" I had it once by heart… "Forlorn!

the very word is like a bell," and ruth
and grief are synonyms of sorts. The night
is dense with them—loved relatives and friends
who, gone by day, are agents of a twilight
state, deep spies who tout a counter truth
and shadow us until the grieving ends.

THE GOOD LIFE (A DREAM)

Relaxing on lawn chairs beside the Jordan
River, we take in a lecture on how
in the olden days some clever Roman found
papyrus strips encrusted with sand
and baked hard by the sun, and thus brought forth
Sheetrock. And I ask my friend Dave if he's
ever wondered how many discoveries
and nifty inventions of great worth

must have accrued over the eons
for us to lounge in comfort here today.
Amazing, he agrees. Then, drawing near to
the river, I thrust my foot in, thinking, *Lo—
this is it, that most blessèd of streams,*
as my soul flares up and I am blown away.

UNDER YUCATAN

A gap in the jungle floor without
a marker, but pushing the bushes
aside—"This cave is about to be
famous," says our guide, leading us down
a rusted ladder to a pool we
wade through in our wetsuits, then around
a corner: spikes and needles of rock
and a massive limestone column blinking
with bats, mid-lake. "The rock is fragile,
please don't touch," he tells us, as we stroke
and splash beyond the column, dipping
under open-eyed where blind fish dart
within a blue so fiendishly trans-
parent we can see their beating hearts.
We drift and paddle, awed, lose touch with
the bottom, dive and swim among the fish,
whose souls we can almost see, if fish
had souls. "Look up." Our guide directs his
flare at the roof's repeating zigzag
hex, a figure seared by lamp-oil near
a sheltered ledge stained red. What rites, what
blood-lettings happened here? He shakes his head.
"Now make a circle please, turn off your lamps."

*

*My mother dead, and
   friends and cousins gone.
  Those hapless towers
trashed, long wars begun,
   unending twisted
times, always the future*

   *like a scroll of necessary
  chances that we stumble
into, blind as fish*

*in caves we can't
swim out of, caged in
 labyrinths of loss.*

     ★

He turns his lamp on and we fill our lungs,
blink, sucked back into light's bright gift of
presence, greet each other, parents, children,
friends, these cherished apparitions, caught
in time's intractable embrace.

MT. TAMALPAIS
for Nancy

> *"When an excursion is proposed, all sorts of dangers are conjured up, filling the wilderness with Indians, bears, snakes, bugs, impassable rivers, and jungles of brush, to which is always added quick and sure starvation."*
>
> John Muir *(Picturesque California, 1888)*

Beyond the firehouse, past the water
tower, the old trail thins and darkens.
Starbursts and lupines, bluebells, as we
climb (Aline your cousin, you, me, Ben
nineteen) toward the rustic string of cabins
Ali summered at when she was small.
We meet a guy who's hiking to the coast.
And what will he do there? Ali inquires.
Just camp and watch for whales. Last year by
the ocean, I recall, we saw a big-
eyed octopus blanch white and move in
on a white anemone, caressing
with suckered tentacles the lovely
plant-like beast, which shrank back on its rock,
drew in its fronds, and sat there like a
squishy volleyball. Cross-species love
is not assured of course. Reaching the homely
lodge we greet the resident tabby, break
out picnic lunch and you recount how Ben,
last spring, racked by another seizure,
fell and one plastic tooth came loose, then
heading for the dentist got confused,
phoned home and we pulled out our map.
He read us street names, we said take a left.
(In the age of the cell phone you can't
get totally lost.) Ben has a Coke,
I buy a hot chai tea, while you and
Aline share some bottled fizz, and we

head down. Suddenly weaving across
our path, these copulating dragonflies—
he rides on her back, tail curled under
like a teacup handle. They sally by,
a sampan gliding on a lake, come
gracefully about and pass again,
a breath away. But later that afternoon
at Max's retro 50s-style cafe
with Fats & Elvis on the mini-juke,
Ben complains his faulty memory
screws him up at school. Back in fifth grade,
each flag and capital, and all the books
he'd read were easy to recall but now
scarred neurons block key sectors of his
brain, new facts evaporate and solids
turn to mush. He squints into this absence
of yesterdays, an attic of empty shelves,
the tyranny of *now*. It drives you
frantic with a parent's tangled love,
but shaky on the past he plays his
violin with skill and looks ahead
with humor and ripe moods that make him
still himself. Remember
L.A. on that winter break, we'd seen
La Brea and the Rodin show, and
on our sixteenth anniversary
you took the tiger seed into your womb,
a deed of blood and of desire. Something
from nothing when the semen took. Whatever
turned up, we would live with that. The mind
strays through these primal woods, impossible
to say I am this thing that was, trails
winding among shadow with no final
destination we can name. Big ones
come down and block the path and rot and feed
the soil. O fabulous legends, captious distances!
We wander here together in the dusk.

THE ATTACK

As I ambled down-yard
toward the strawberry patch
where berries bunched

like tiny pink seed pearls,
it snatched at my hair, raking
the skin beneath with

needle claws, thinking it
had bagged a perfect source for
nest making or even a whole

ready-made nest wafting
past bluebells and wild roses
through its yard, and when

my brazen hand grazed by,
shouting a raucous *"Dee-dee-
dee-DEE!"* in my ear as if

I had no right to my own hair,
reluctantly the insolent
black-capped thug let loose
and flitted back into the spruce.

THE UNSAFE HOUSE

Waking after the dream to a slick
December gloom (a threat of end-time
hovers around the room), he goes
over the escape route, knowing the
attackers, a posse of children
with rifles and machetes, could smash
down the closet door, and find his
family huddled there, then finish them off
with a few brisk rounds to the head.
Better instead to scramble up through
the ceiling access way and into
the space below the canted roof
where they might go undetected,
and as he sits up and starts to dress—
a sickle moon slash-sinister in
the west—it comes to him that they
can make it up there using the bureau drawers
        for steps
                and closing
                        them behind,
so that once they've replaced the sheetrock
ceiling door they could wait it out in that
unlit frigid space. But they'll need extra
sweaters—*hurry, for God's sake hurry!*—
as the enemy rabble is breaking
into the house like they do, it seems,
on a daily basis in those far-off
desperate places where justice and
mercy have lost their cachet and life
holds much less value than in our dreams.

HOMELESS IN SEATTLE

Slouched in front of Bartell Drugs,
resting her chin on a man-sized crutch,
hat pulled down, she dozes where

yesterday standing tall, she laughed
and razzed the passersby, living on
that tattered edge you walk past fast

fists in pockets, cross the road
to where he sits legs stretching out
in sandaled feet and skews your path

under the painted yellow arch
asking for "the price of a Mac
in change" who yesterday you saw

slip behind that bush to pee. And this
unnerving youth with hair as long
as yours, a glint of jagged teeth,

who comes at you arms wide, hands
crooked and fingers pointing down—
"Get down!" he yells (you circle round),

"What the fuck you doin'? *Fuck!*"
Living solo at the invalids' hotel,
hot flashes, no libido, diarrhea,

sleeping not so well (rude facts
that overrun your fate), each
day for the allotted spell you lie

beneath a plastic artifice of sky
whose faded summer lakeside blue
you gaze at drifting in and out of time

while the clattering machine
slings its life-affirming rays that
take your raging prostate tumors down.

CELESTIAL FIRESTORM

Its green arc flares, swings low, crinkles, snaps
while stars behind glint through like sequins on
a shawl. *Where does it come from?* he asks.
                              The sun,
you say, *I think,* pull onto the shoulder and step
out into chill. *But we only see it at
night. Does it happen in daytime too and we
just can't see?* It riffles, billows, flaps
like a pennant although there is no breeze.

His eyes dilated, dazzled by this binge
of fractiousness beyond our steady state,
plumb a strange new paradigm of space.
Drawing back, it slings a swarm of arrows tinged
with pink. You duck. It points a warning finger:
Look out, mortals, things could get much worse.

POSTCARD FROM NANCY

As companion to the Crivelli, a Vermeer
with your sad hand full
of worries on the reverse. This
too from the Gardner:

a young Dutch lady performs at the virginal.
A gallant gentleman, his
back to us, lends one ear
to the music, while

his other attends a blue dressed matron's
account. Inevitably
the checkerboard floor; and
in the left foreground

a bass viol had been laid down next
to a draped desk.
Is he a soldier?
Beside the quill

and parchment, could it be that those
are coins? Why
in such a domestic
scene does Caravaggio's

prostitute laugh on the wall above the music?
This painting filled
with lightly arrested motions
may offer us repose,

in hope that, not in despite of the world,
our music, when I
escort your viola, will hold
us counterpoised.

My diamond for his guilders? No. No brokers, Nancy.
In this age of
war and purchased love
mine's a free answer.

Iowa City, 1965

II.

ANALECTS
(a gathering of literary fragments)

ANALECTS OF THE RED CANOE

*"Greedy for happiness, which he saw as an endless
succession of sunny afternoons..."*—Proust

Sparks slide on the water, leap up
like fire stirred with a stick, as we heft
   the canoe over boulders into the bobbing
current.
        A neon flash of insect wings,
and around us downtown Fairbanks, Sunday,

     pushing noon—a log church steeple sheathed
in metal, and the gaudy purple Chena View Hotel.
Sweatshirts stowed under seats, Nancy
   steers at the stern:
              "Warn me if you
see rocks." At the bow my knuckles scrape

the side. Beneath—dissolving branches,
   rocks, the slime on which the river glides
eliding fact and
         looking, as our four orange
   life jackets sluice beneath a bridge
where lovers sketched bold deeds on gray concrete.

Ben waves to a passing green inflated raft
   and resting lady double-kayakers. Gnats,
mosquitoes,
          dragonflies. Grass and
willows sparse on the muddy banks,
   as I trail my fingers in a melt of

      glacial implications sliding toward
some vaster chill. Iced to the wrist,
I wipe them on my pants.
                      A swallow spins
on sharp wingtips shaping effortless
    foliations in fast flight, and soon

the power plant, a steel-blue grizzly
    rampant on our left. Coal cars to
the right, while just
                    above us coal chunks,
scuttling, ride a screened-in belt across.
"Look, Ben," I point, recalled by the stench

    of ash to Rockaway: black barges docked
beside Jamaica Bay where another power plant
rising from
                  infancy vents its paternal
rage. The inward mind's not thought itself
    but shapes the senses resonate in matter—

tangible spirit—nerve taking on a new
    design, as wandering its grid of town,
the river carves an eighth dimension.
Lit from below the
                bridges shimmy; backyards
    sprout their primary swing-set patios

the avenues concealed, and the legal
    artifice of lots breaks down. Whose tabby
lounges on whose cord of wood, stacked
    between car-ports? The buzz
                        of a float-plane
fades, and the roar of something raw around

            the bend ripples the river's chronic afternoon.
Two speedboats dash up-current. Jeffrey
     calls out, adding his
                    weight to the roll,
as Nancy yells, "Sit still!" seeking our balance
     in their chilly wake. And, churning, I remember

     Guy Lombardo racing on Jamaica Bay when
I was three. I saw him
                    flip his boat
and spit out flame, I saw his nearly mortal shape
lifted to sirens up and
                    carried limp away.

Sun flashes a sandbox, a plastic loader, pots,
     and trucks: you know the castle in your games
has such a moat—
               sluggish, cold, and filled
with glamorous teeth. Why mope—this world is
     so damn full of menace: even a rabbit, Ben,

or a canoe. Like an infestation of stigmata,
     gnats, blue and luminous, drift above a glare
of discordant sensations:
                    brown icy water
under the brightest sun glazing our skins. Jeffrey
takes a paddle and joins in. Ben
                         rows with a stick.

Ducks in a small cove nervously watch us go.
     No houses now on the banks, just grassy fields
with fireweed and vetch.
               Even before its
     roar, a massive Japan jet in front of us
takes off—grows small. And in its softening wake,

the hum of water on the hull, a swish of paddles,
   voice of a child who tells himself about
the shells of robins and of snails.
                                      Occasional
traffic rumbles, shouts, the rhythmic tapping
   of a distant tape-deck. Amid the random music

     of what is, the family in canoe turns restless,
then relaxes, paddles,
                     rests, and finds it has no
destination it can name. Just here, just
                               now, under one
   specific, sheep-shaped cloud, the pastoral afternoon
becomes itself. We drift into our contrapuntal lives.

And drowsing I perceive him—scraggly bearded,
   dressed in torn old corduroys and patched
plaid shirt:
          a counter-self who missed the channel,
   got mired in some dead-end slough. He fled the draft
to Canada and then to Fairbanks—comes to himself

at forty-four, a hunter, trapper, not at home
   with other men. Alone in his barn, everything
logged to one side: books
                     on a legless couch
beside a jug, a hotplate, the half-unfinished kennel
   akimbo on its pick-up. So easy
                               to come apart—

   just liquor and pills and floating pains that
stun him in the night. He
                    lies on his back
   and watches the ceiling crawl. How fragile
the skin of today? And no one
                        brave enough to face
what nature's maker really thinks of us,

invaders of the air. Our traffics of corruption
    ooze along the curb. Out in the yard, trees
charred where fire gripped
                              their bark surround
a flowery emptiness. Ragweed climbs its stem.
Our tissues are not chosen, we do with them

what we can. The kind domestic gentleman
    contains this killer whom he covers up and
cares for in his dreams. But once
                                last winter,
walking the a.m. dark through ice-fog,
he felt his cage come open, having reached

    a new design remoteness, fog and freeze were
part of—a clean escape from
                              wanting too much love.
Snow turning gray toward dawn, a thin white cat
crouched on the hood of a truck. He
                        struck a match
    and watched it flare, burn, blacken, die as smoke.

His name is gone,
                dissolved, and in another season
I wake on the Chena in the red canoe, just as
    the paddle-wheeler
                      named "Discovery II" looms
over us. From three high decks, a lovely white and
    blue, tourists gawk down and wave as Ben waves back.

Then into its sudden wake, we dive and roll.
    Convulsing peaks and troughs we—rocking—
muddle through,
            together, threatened, contemplating
shore—a sodden swim. Perhaps we'd make it, shaken
    and chilled raw. "Hold on," I shout, "stay low!"

My pulse begins to slow, and now my Polish
     grandmother hovers over this. A great dark shape
when I was four, she carried
                    me out and
dropped me seething in. I felt my panic grow
     beneath the Atlantic's
                         salt and spit, unlikely fish,

flapping toward sandy ground. As everything falls
crisply to its spot, the river,
                         calming, brings in focus
     all my obstinate shores. In mid-career, the heart
tempers its beat, you switch from beef to fowl,
     from anger to a gentler disaffection. Now, if ever,

you must catch your early purpose, stitch it to
     your chest like a tattoo. The mast, the manatee,
the mutineer become
                    your emblems—those images of
water and the past. The branch of a skinny aspen
     floating by, Jeffrey leans halfway out and hauls

     it in, dousing his brother. Benjamin throws
a fit. I shift him to my seat,
                    stand, stretch,
sit, and, starting to lie back...almost before I see
     it go—what might have been a fish, caught
in the shore-weeds, branches, belly up. I thought

I glimpsed a face, white, bloated, bobbing past.
     A blood-drained salmon floating in a pool?
The look and smell of fish. Or—was it?—an
                              old drunk,
lost, who stumbled in and drowned, got carried from
     downtown to where the Chena bends, and found

the shore, snagged in a sweeper, resting on his back.
    Time stipples, bubbles, fizzes.
                                I tell myself,
        that old man was a fish, and then dismiss
the thought, knowing
                    I'll worry later what I've done.

Breaking apart, you gather up the shards of your
decay and puzzle till an
                    edge defines its match,
    paddle till your shoulders take on paddling
as their mission
                and reward you with a piece of self.

The river swinging south, sweepers brush by.
    Against a longer view, Mt. Deborah and Mt. Hess,
white breasts among the clouds, appear and
disappear, and then another,
                        greater river
    plucks us like a twig and sweeps us west.

A spinning fish-wheel passes quickly. Speed
lifts us out of torpor. "Watch out, sit and be still!"—
    Nancy alerts the kids. The Tanana means business.
Its glacial grit
            abrades the hull. The surface
like a horizontal curtain in the wind, knotted

then smooth, then flexing like the muscles of
    a gray young body dancing. I clutch a kicking paddle
and my knuckles hum.
                    We sight on a sandy spit
where tents and motorhomes sit toylike, dogs and
    children scamper. The river,
                            sectioned, eddies,

    flows, dead spots a darker gray, and far as the eye
goes west, the sun leans on an elbow big enough
to drink the river up.
                      Above, five wavering
gulls; ahead, a green flat-bottomed airboat
    blasting hard against the current. Black stunted

spruce on the flats, gray hills, and whiteness
    in the range. A sudden
                      happiness in things
that pins us to this place. The house we've built
appears above us, shapely
                  on its ridge, as the airboat,

splashing, cuts
           across our bow, and giddily
  we're doused and shouting at the long end of
this alabaster day. The afternoon,
                              not fragments,
finally, but sitting still and moving in the mind

of this old badger, or like some northern crockery
    with fireweed for border. And pulling in to shore—
a yard, a car on blocks, refrigerator
                        rusting on its side—
    this quiet moment looking down through silt:
one orange stone and countless petals of light.

III.
HISTORIES

ELISABETH VIGÉE-LEBRUN (1755-1842): SELF-PORTRAIT

A peasant hat set back, long hair let down—
and for five minutes at a time your

eyes are held by mine, and by my lips'
slight part. I practiced an art

without shadows, each pigment in a brighter mode,
and I looked as good as my portraits

in those days. How fine
to have a wife so gifted, pretty, smart,

but he abused my art
and gambled the money away. I hid

the jewels. But when he ruffled me one time
too many I packed my case

and made my way to court,
a life I might have sunk in

like the goose-down mattress on my bed,
but something in me said

a woman's luck can change.
I had a trade while all the excellence around me

knew only how to ride, to speak, to dance.
I lived to paint,

and even on the morning of my daughter's birth
worked in my studio

between the pains. What joy
to trace their diaphanous hair,

the wistful lace at their wrists.
So few of my paintings please me

fully even now, but you must admit
my blues and pinks are not insipid.

No man could do as much. Few worked
as hard or loved the monarchy as I.

One night I saw my husband at a ball. Laughing,
I removed his wig and wiped

the powder from his blushing face. I put a sheet
around him for a toga, crowned him

with a wreath, a theme
that leapt from court to town, the Greek

age come again. Oh but all the paint
in Paris could not save the queen.

They had a guillotine
for me. I saw one head cut off

and carried on a pike. We fled
by coach that night through the cruel

impoverished streets, and
ate just gruel and bread crust

for the three disordered weeks
we jounced to Italy.

Unlike the ill-tempered wealth
that follows, they were knowledgeable, chic,

and—often—sympathetic, but it took a poet's
art to show what wanted to be seen.

Especially the queen. I loved her,
loved her gentlemen and ladies, who also

lost their heads and I cursed my Roman
comforts in those days of

bloody strife, as the tragic news came in—
one after another of my famous sitters

dead. I'd seen them for all time, not
flattering or false, but

as if in a moment of
surprising natural beauty,

alive today if paint
could heal the razored heartbeats of a life.

"A-CRANBERRYING"
from Thoreau's journal

Though he foresaw "a lame conclusion" to
his walk, he noted that plans you have
low expectations for often surprise you,

since intuition like the vibrant whir of
news on a hummingbird's wing may veer beyond
the commonplace—as at the modest shack

he'd built beside the not-yet-famous pond
just a short stroll down the Fitchburg track
from home. So putting his politic worries

to one side, he departs his usual sphere,
crosses Great Field to Beck Stow's Swamp, where,
to his delight, large clusters of cranberries

raft like red foam on the sphagnous flood,
removes his shoes and socks and wades into mud.

A RENAISSANCE ALTARPIECE

Uccello painted them: a family bound
together to a tree-trunk post, staring
with horror down as flames leap up from
foot to calf to knee. Four horsemen on
the right display the flag of Rome. Across
from them, with faces glistening in the flame-
light, stand the helmeted guards who
trussed this family up and set them blazing.

Two boys, both red heads, share their parents'
fate, while in the background—fields, a leafy
apple tree, farm houses, and a church.
The sky behind a neighbor castle town
is black. The merchant and his pregnant wife
and boys were damned for what they did to
desecrate the host. "Religion," I once
told a Catholic friend, "makes good people better,

bad people worse." Another panel illustrates
their crime. They cooked it in a pan until
it bled. The blood of Christ spilled out and ran
across the floor, and when it dribbled
underneath the door, they were exposed.
Have you ever fallen from the second
story window of a dream—the broken
glass, the silent floating scream? You'd think

at least the child in her womb could be
redeemed. Why would a Jewish merchant
be so hostile to the host? Why in
Urbino was this credited? What calculus
of feeling can elucidate this art, unless
it charts a program to annihilate
a race. Aghast, the baffled victims
stare at lizard flames that leap and leap.

COUNTING CARIBOU— PRUDHOE BAY, ALASKA
after R. Glendon Brunk

Tundra to the horizon peppered with lakes,
aswim with pintails and loons. A fox lopes by.
The sky's aslant with jaegers, rough-legged hawks.
I'm paid to tally caribou, a science guy.

Behind me a maze of pipes, pumps, drill-
pads, gravel pits, and sludge-smudged drums,
and everywhere the reek of corporate oil.
But hey, I'm here to count the herd, which comes

(if they come at all) too fast to count, then mill
when they hit the pipe. They mass and twitch, until
one coast-bound leader steps up, lifts her muzzle,
sniffs, while baffled calves and mothers nuzzle,
just as a truck roars by, blaring its god-
damn horn and they stampede away. I hate this job!

ABOVE THE TANANA: FOR JERRY CABLE

1. APRIL, 1988

I squint into the morning's brilliance—
sun on ice at sixty degrees warm. Beyond

the ledge the river holds its form,
but you have left us for some grimmer place.

The other day I thought I saw your face.
At the wheel of a pick-up you pulled out of

the Pumphouse heading home. I know the mind
can play such tricks, unwilling or unable

to let go. Behind me, Spirit's pawing the dry
leaves. I hear her collar jingle but keep mum.

Out of the west two Phantom bombers come:
like tandem wasps they home in on their base.

Mt. Hayes is hazy, Deborah lost in clouds.
I summon back your dying year of verse,

no loss of power in its quirky grace. Then Martha's
whispered message on the phone: "It won't be long."

We saw the lights one midnight from your place,
a lovely sky-show—blooms and tendrils

constantly born and dying out in space—
whose abstract beauty served to keep us warm.

No flowers yet, no sap smell from the trees.
Crossing the ice—the giant shadow of a bird.

I look into the sun, seeking its source.
My eyes go liquid and my mind goes numb.

2. ONE YEAR LATER

A second winter plays out its strong hand.
Jerry—as pain grows less and bitter knowledge

more, I can't forget you in your dying year—
the bold words coming as your drugs allowed

their odd, particular humor, their angular warmth.
When I arrived through drifts at this clear,

rooted spot, a six dog sled was loping by.
Watching their avid speed, I thought about

your progress into dust—what part of air
you are. What other shore has your increase

of wisdom in decay released you to? Near tundra
yesterday, I drove northeast from town; a raven and

a rough-legged hawk fought on the road. The silver
bird flew up and hovered, while the dark one

hopped and fluttered into brush. At 3 a.m. a bloody
wash lacquered the southern sky. I felt complicit

with its morbid chemistry. Perhaps it's just
the vanity of art that rips through muscle

to expose the heart? You knew such qualms.
Those dogs looked happy in the brilliant haze.

The driver was absorbed by her soft ride.
Pulled by my words, I follow into wish—

a rune, a riddle some lost persona utters
that will not be forgotten in the rush

of what we are into what
isn't us and couldn't care.

3. A SECOND YEAR

The brown leaves rattle on a cottonwood.
No crocuses, no rose buds, but the snow

begins to vacate this secluded spot,
and sun sparks through the spruce. Jerry,

last night at a banquet in your honor
as you sat across from me, silent while

purple phrases bloomed into bright porphyry
that surely would have faded on the page,

when my turn came no words occurred.
Could silence honor you like poetry?

At least you were still living in my dream.
Awake, I know you're buried in your home county,

but we can talk. Indulge my fantasy.
I'd like to fill you in. Those Russian verbs

you sweated might prove useful after all,
with Eastern Europe under democratic rule

and Bering Strait these days quite crossable.
You know about the killings in the Sound,

dead birds, sea otters, seals, dead everything.
You shake your head in fury and your sickened

face turns red. I hear you crying, "Shit
on Alyeska!" for the spill. You worked

the arctic slope and know those
creeps would stop at nothing to make dough.

A mottled gray on white of passing clouds
flows on the ice. Our friends agree that

you still hang around, part of the air,
part of the supple ground. At least what's

in me doesn't ache as much, though there's an absence
like an organ that's been cut. Another

season's passing and I need to keep in touch.

4. STILL REMEMBERING

A greening jasper in the slough as water
pushes up. The hillside's sage—

I pluck a sprig, rub it between
my fingers for its aromatic breath

recalling the fragrant teas you kept
in packs—Earl Grey and Lapsang—scattered

around your place the year when you lived humbly
in a one room shack on a downtown Fairbanks street

and Martha studied out of state. I'd cycle
by to visit, drink your bourbon, share

your tapes of poets, exchange views. Does James
Wright's work go sentimental in the end?

You said it was too easy to get drunk
at the Dog or the Boatel, the local dives,

and come back stinking, flushed, needing
to straighten out and write. You'd crash

the whole next day. Thank god for poetry,
you said, to keep us sane. I stop and wonder,

am I crazy to go on with you like this?
Say it: he's dead, and nothing could be worse.

But as I rise to go a raven flashes up croa-
croaking from the island just offshore.

He yells and circles, dives, swings by, and
floats on down the slough, then turns again—

a black hole on the sky that whirls me
in its almost human eye, a voice

as desperate and playful as your verse.

ASK LOUISE

Even the love letters disappoint—
too innocent and dear amid
their dust and one cent stamps.
From the heart of Indiana
with Louise, you brought them back

and at your sister's house we unpack
cartons, read their faded hands.
This formalized regret for 'Sam,'
a son now dead no matter what:
"may scripture give thee comfort."

Timid Louise—surprise—had bought a Dodge
and taught herself to drive at sixty-five.
And this from New Orleans—"We've
few Friends here, thy faith is wanting"—
chills me with vast differences. We pass

the sugar tongs and bowl with purple
tarnish hatched two centuries back,
ponder initials on the florid silverware,
and polish a serving spoon to a soft
sheen to glass its curlicues: *A. S.*

And these pince-nez—too quaint!
We thumb through photos for the odd
resemblances. Whose riding camp was this
with distant cousins caught
in happy genteel pre-war poses

too stiff to be believed? Or else—
let's ask Louise. I wonder will they
box our things like this, toss most,
and salvage what holds value
in an age when overcrowding's certain,

winter doubtful. Is longevity assured?
Last week Louise, our link, moved
to a home. She can't depose the evidence
we've plundered. Phew—pink polish stinks.
Shaky with absences we pack it up.

INTO MY HEAD
after Frigyes Karinthy

A squeal of bit on bone that opens up
my skull. A sucking sound as liquids drain
from ventricles, linked lakes inside the brain.
Strapped on my stomach to the tabletop,

I seem to rise above him, float apart,
and watch him lift cracked bones out with gloved hands,
then split the lobes and stare, while I assess his art.
He palms the insidious fruit with crimson strands

twining around, a curse, an adverse jewel
growing inside, which brings on nonstop night
and the clatter of trains that rattles me out of
myself until I hardly know what's real.
He bites his lip and lops the canker out.
"Cheer up, old mole," he says. "With luck you'll live."

TWO VIEWS OF THE WRECKAGE
for the artist, Kes Woodward

Note: Climate change models show interior Alaska becoming dryer while coastal areas flood worldwide.

Kibitzing over your shoulder as you
sketch those billowing clouds above the
staved-in houseboat in its dried up slough,
I sense the berrying bear that ambled by a
day or two ago leaving this gritty substance,
fear, like a pheromone, hanging there
and there—and because we codgers share
a wish to buck the laws of change and chance

you cache the present scene while I flash on
distant glittering Venice seen back when
the band played gaudy Liszt and Beethoven
and Sputnik shimmered over St Mark's Square
where now high waters climb the palace stair
as ice-sheets thaw and toxic tides roll in.

SOUNDS IN A FOREST

Between the inlet and the gated homes,
this bike path—muddy, tree-shadowed, with
the heavy scent of loam—while off to our left
a great blue heron perches on a rock, and
overhead Ben spots an osprey nest. He rides
a yellow three-wheeled Terratrike, low
to the ground in case a seizure strikes.

Then as we circle back a splitting sound
sharp as a whip-crack splinters through the woods
where maples, oaks, and chestnuts arch, and then
a stairstep stutter, "cra…cra…craa…craa…craa"
like something big's about to fall on us.
Are we the butt of nature's sly retort
to Berkeley's two-faced riddle of design?

And in that moment's indecision—
should we flee or wait out the conclusion,
the way things happen in the *now*—a child's
sickness or a parent's passing, buildings charred
to rubble, planes gone down—who's left to say,
if a big-leaf maple tree uproots and
lands on top of us, what sound occurred?

Philosophy is empty here. A nest's sweet
fissure where the eggs were laid, a slug's
retreat, a squirrel's stomping ground may
come to grief, as I recall my last night's dream—
in a flooding house, we hurried up the stairs
and saw through gutted roof the clouds
like spigots pouring inspiration down.

And then it happens—an object sonorous
with leaves slapping past leaves, its bark rasping
past other limbs, and all those minor intricate lives
dependent on that branch, flummoxed,
must pack up and move to other digs
as all my stale beliefs come floating like
a cancelled midnight stanza from the sky.

AMERICAN TALIBAN

Because of divorce he sought
wholeness, because of affluence,
poverty. Inflexible diversity
drove him toward uniformity,
though if he'd been truly violent,
he'd have put on a uniform.

Drawn to his local mosque
by the flatteries of prayer,
he fell on his knees toward Mecca,
and took up a new fidelity,
then making his way to Yemen,
joined in an antique reading

of the text, which speeds from
the Prophet's hand straight to
the eyes and heart of man. As hair
and beard grew wild, he mixed with
the sons of tribesmen, no longer
a skittish child, and girded himself

to fight. We saw him the other night,
carried from the cellar of the bloody
Afghan fortress and met our own
confusion in his swooning,
sleepless eyes, but hidden in their
wounded animation, cocked grenades

beneath a turban, were the fateful
words of Allah, merging camels
and commotion, the Covenant and
Gospels, donkeys drowned in
swirling waters in the land-locked
land of Omar, doubtful nation,

where devotion haunts the part of
us we squander when we batten
down or knuckle under and
calls upon that goodness which
created us in stages—called by us,
like Noah, "*God-possessed.*"

THE ASSIGNMENT: HARVARD, 1962

*The sedge has wither'd from the lake
And no birds sing*

A gray afternoon. I lay on my
bed, like a gun aimed at a target
with no one to pull the trigger.
There was an ocean with ripples
and waves and an occasional

seabird far in the distance and I
rose and fell with the swell of it,
deep in the belly of not wanting.
So dinnertime passed as I lay there
with the assignment, due the next day,

undone. Hectoring thoughts whirled
through me like hailstones—this was
the end of freedom, the end of
happiness—as the hours passed and
misery lashed me with her whip.

I dozed briefly and lurched
awake with frayed nerves and
clammy skin. It was winter,
bare trees, birds gone south,
and something inside me was broken.

I'd come to the end of childhood
in the grip of a monstrous fear
that I might be turning into someone
I wouldn't even like—some twit,
dull, snotty, bookish, and dry.

Next day, I got up around noon,
splashed water on my face,

dragged myself to my desk, and
did it, and at the very last minute
turned it in. Had anything changed?

Not really. For months after,
I kept looking in on myself like
a nurse on a sickly patient, taking
the weak pulse of my feelings,
fearing a relapse, until one day

I glanced out the window and saw
down in the courtyard the bright
yellow blooms of forsythia
and felt my bruised core mending,
as my heart rattled back to life.

THE UNNAMED LAKE

*In memory of Charles Ott and William Ruth,
Denali Park photographers*

Slogged over tipsy muskeg, past a "moose
wallow," grizzly tracks, to reach this breeze-
rippled lake, where, through waving horsetails,
a golden-eye, her pesky offspring in tow,

preens and dives. Across the sky-flecked water, spruce,
then tundra meadows mount toward jagged Zs
of rock. Like specks of white-out, Dall sheep line
the ridge. If this place had a name, it's been

erased, in homage to two men whose ashes
seed the hills nearby. They staked their lives
on wildness beyond naming. Can we go back,
reclaim the power of unaltered place? Blue
and luminous, a damselfly lights on this page;
two kingfishers weigh in, wheel off down the lake.

DENALI PARK FALL DRIVE-THROUGH

This roadside nature was once
wilderness, which now boasts
campsites, toilets, rangers, rows
of split-log benches by the lake.

By the lake loud honks and squeaks,
a skyey tumult. We look up
where specks by the dozens swirl
like streamers, sink, form rippling Vs,

then lift and vanish into air as
hundreds more, riding the thermals,
circle toward Denali's mass, a
vast white humpback whale set off

by craggy pyramids too tall for
cranes to top. How thrilling,
operatic, this sky teeming with
birds blown in from the lonely tundra

to greet the turning season—a frenzied,
festive, taxis-in-Times-Square
cacophony of cranes! One red capped pair
skims low, long-necked, hooked

beaks like spears with spindly
trailing legs, then catching an
updraft, rise into the sky's blue
brilliance seeking passage through.

PSALM (AFTER NIETZSCHE)

That day is coming soon when our people,
all the cousins, pets, children
will begin to disperse like the insects
of summer after the petals fall.
And where do they go, those bees,

those dragonflies? Into the soil
where they break into pieces, a wing,
an antenna, a thorax, absently dreaming
of spring, as the long cold settles over
them, their buzzing and sipping forgotten.

And a great age passes like those
lumbering eras we learned of
in grade school, or the unbelievable time
it takes to make a star and its planets and
evolve a living world—all gone to ground,

and trillions of years slip by in silence
under the earth, but then one day, one
millennium, a gentle humming and something
oozing, gripping, reaching, this relentless longing
toward light—urgent, fantastic. It could happen.

JOHN MORGAN studied with Robert Lowell at Harvard, where he won the Hatch Prize for Lyric Poetry. At the Iowa Writers Workshop, he earned an MFA and was awarded the Academy of American Poets Prize. In 1976, Morgan moved with his family to Alaska, where for many years he directed the Creative Writing Program at the University of Alaska Fairbanks. His poems have appeared in *The New Yorker*, *Poetry*, *The American Poetry Review*, *The New Republic*, *The Paris Review*, and many other magazines. In 2009, he served as the first writer-in-residence at Denali National Park. Annie Dillard writes that Morgan's poems "are strong and full of carefully controlled feeling. They are tender and precise evocations of the moral and sensory life of man."